St David's School, Wrexham

— a collection of pictures

Other titles in the *Collection of Pictures* series

St David's School, Wrexham

— a collection of pictures

W. Alister Williams

bridge
books

St David's School, Wrexham — a collection of pictures
First published in Wales in 2003
by
Bridge Books
61 Park Avenue
Wrexham
LL12 7AW

© 2003 W Alister Williams

ISBN 1-84494-001-2

A CIP catalogue entry for this book is
available from the British Library

*Items that are printed in this style are genuine answers given by
pupils in answer to examination or test questions. While the Humanities subjects
lend themselves to this type of error, no subjects were exempt. One answer —about the
Prodigal Son— actually ended up as a line on Benny Hill's TV show in the 1980s.
These items were collected over many years by Mr Gwynne Belton.*

Certain teachers have been provided with very short pen portraits to accompany
photographs. These do not in any way indicate a higher level of recognition for
a particular member of staff but, rather, simply provide added details where
the illustration would seem to warrant it. Many equally deserving teachers
have not been included in this way simply because a suitable
photograph was not available.

Printed and bound by
Ashford Colour Press
Hampshire

Introduction

Despite a world preoccupied by the horrors of the Second World War, by 1943 there was little doubt in anyone's mind that the conflict would eventually result in an Allied victory. Most politicians were giving time to planning what sort of society would emerge from the conflict and all agreed that the economic depression of the 1930s, with its resulting poverty and failing health provisions, must be avoided at all costs. Although formed in 1939 to prosecute the war against Germany, the Coalition government was ideally placed to consider the future on bi-partisan lines. While most students of 20th century British history would readily accept that the post-war Labour government of 1945–51 was probably the most revolutionary in terms of the implementation of new policies, few would fail to recognise the important role played by its predecessor. In terms of health, the Beveridge Report (headed by the Liberal Sir William Beveridge) laid the foundations for the development of the National Health Service in 1948 and, likewise, in the field of education, the 1944 Education Act (formulated under the leadership of Conservative R. A. Butler) cast the dye which influenced education philosophy for the second half of the century. St David's School, Wrexham, was the direct product of the 1944 Act.

St David's, in addition to having been an example of educational thinking for the past fifty-years, managed to carve a special place for itself in the community which it served. Starting from scratch, the school established an enviable reputation for high standards in both academic and pastoral education. It has been said that when the school opened the headmaster and staff were determined that 'secondary modern' did not mean 'second class'. From the outset there was an ethos about the school which permeated into every nook and cranny, into every pupil and teacher. In later years, with the introduction of comprehensive education, St David's slipped quietly into the mantle that had previously been worn by Grove Park School; its standards of excellence had already been well established and the absorption of those pupils who would previously have gone to the grammar school was carried out without major difficulty.

I was fortunate to have been appointed to the staff of St David's in the final years of Gareth Williams' headship and quickly realised that I had joined a very successful and happy team. The school had a reputation for achieving standards that were considerably beyond the national average in terms of both academic results and extra-curricular activities. St David's was a name that was well known throughout north Wales and its pupils and staff were proud to belong to such a successful establishment.

I would like to take this opportunity to thank everyone who has contributed towards the production of this book. To list them all would be impossible. I just hope that the finished product rekindles fond memories.

W Alister Williams
Asst. Teacher of Humanities, 1976–80
Head of History/Deputy Head of Humanities, 1980–90

St David's Secondary School/ Ysgol Uwchradd Dewi Sant

St David's Secondary Modern School, Wrexham, built by the then Denbighshire Education Authority, was the first new secondary school to be constructed in this expanding Welsh town since the War.

In comparison with buildings in the Borough which had given valiant service for very many years, it could be described as palatial. Aesthetically, with its beautiful site, range of colour schemes, light airy classrooms and distant views of the Welsh hills beyond its excellent 20 acre playing fields and the towers and spires of Wrexham, this lovely modern building suggested unlimited possibilities and ensured an environment which, if used wisely, could provide only contentment and happiness.

The challenge was a serious one! And so, on the morning of September 2nd 1957, the first assembly took place of 544 pupils of whom 364 were boys and 205 were girls, together with Headteacher, Deputy Headteacher, Senior Mistress, 26 teachers, part time secretary, caretaker and representatives of the Wrexham Divisional Executive and the Governing Body.

The reading was taken from the 127th Psalm: 'Except the Lord build the house they labour in vain that build it.' An elderly painter from Abergele, busy with his brush and paint on the back wall of the dining stage platform, reverently doffed his hat, there was a slight giggle from a few children as he revealed a bald head, and within a short time the school was on its way.

We as a Staff were to have an increasingly strong realisation that the words of the psalmist would be best achieved by building a school community, rich in the variety of its experiences and actuated by the Christian ideal. A school, after all, was a microcosm of the society it served, — a little world contained within another, displaying all its characteristics.

What was this community which we were to serve?

Geographically, the area containing the children's homes embraced Acton, the whole of the post-war housing estate of Queen's Park as well as Rhosnesni and Marchwiel. It remained so until 1960 when Ysgol Bryn Offa opened in the west of the town.

In terms of human beings, to quote a report by HM Inspectors, 'The school was to provide secondary education for boys and girls who had not qualified for places in the grammar or grammar technical schools, and permitted the reorganisation of three severely overcrowded all-age schools'.

Some pupils entering St David's in September 1957 who had attended the same all-age schools throughout their life, would then remain at St David's for three months and leave at Christmas to find employment in a large and rather harsh world. They were all victims of the infamous 11+ examination.

The serious challenge presented by such factors was to be met by a staff of teachers and ancillaries who understood the needs of the pupils, and who had the educational vision to innovate and provide for them and the skills and qualifications to undertake the task and see it through to a successful conclusion, — namely an education for the child which was rewarding and satisfying. It was fortunate that a team had be recruited which was exceptional in its attitude to the aims of the school and achieved standards in subject teaching which were an inspiration to its pupils. Five years later saw the first successes in GCE 'O' level examinations.

On the other hand, in our desire to build up a school community, 'rich in the variety of its experiences' as expressed earlier, much had to be done outside the normal timetable. Soon there was a growth of school societies and, to quote again reports by HMI — 'one is left with the inescapable impression that the school day had not ended at 3.40pm but that the time had come merely for a different approach to the education of the pupils.'

In addition to the usual sports clubs for football, rugby, hockey, netball, cricket, athletics and cross-country running, regular meetings were held of clubs for crafts, canoe building, beekeeping, ballroom and folk dancing, chess, Scripture Union, Girl Guides, drama, scenery building, record playing, science, Urdd Gobaith Cymru, Duke of Edinburgh's Award, choral and later, bands and orchestra which gained national and international renown.

These were events organised during the school year which saw full productions of: *Midsummer Night's Dream* (who will ever forget Puck and the Dance of the Fairies, later performed on the stage of the Welsh National Eisteddfod at Johnstown); *Toad of Toad Hall* (with the gipsy caravan rolling on to the stage, and the chandeliers with lighted candles, constructed in the metalwork department which caused some consternation when the Wrexham Fire Brigade inspected a performance for safety reasons!). Later followed: *HMS Pinafore, Pirates of Penzance* (twice), *Oliver!* and many superb musical events held at St. Giles Parish Church and the William Aston Hall.

These productions involved staff, a very large number of pupils from all sections of the school who, in addition to acting and singing, made costumes and scenery of professional standards, programmes, tickets and many things necessary for each event.

Visits to industry, places of historic interest, concerts and plays (Stratford on Avon was an annual event) introduced another dimension into the experience of the pupils. Groups also visited Switzerland, Paris, Munich (including Auschwitz), Venice, Lugano and Spain.

Boys and girls spent mountaineering weekends in Snowdonia, attended Urdd camps, competed with reasonable success in competitions involving choral speaking, choirs, folk dancing and even penillion singing in eisteddfodau at Llangollen, Urdd and National level.

Many pupils gained Bronze and Silver medals in the Duke of Edinburgh's award Scheme while two young men and one young lady continued their efforts at the Technical College and were invited to Buckingham Palace for the presentation of the Gold awards.

Participation in various forms of social education was organised and took the form of assistance at local play-groups, helping at Greystones and at homes for the elderly as well as individual cases of old people who lived alone and had little on no social contacts.

Sponsored walks, sales and various activities provided financial assistance for charities with more tangible help such as giving an electric cooker and special tables for the Cheshire Home in the Ceiriog Valley during its early days, and providing parcels for the elderly at Christmas.

Link courses for boys and girls in their final year were provided with the kind co-operation of the principal of the Technical College. These consisted of instruction in motor mechanics, building, welding, for boys and commercial subjects for girls.

We found opportunities for work experience with local firms and these were linked with the development of a Careers Department working in co-operation with the Youth Employment Service.

Academically, the GCE 'O' level courses were quickly gaining ground and providing gratifying results for pupils who had been denied a grammar school education. In 1964/65 we were able to report that eleven out of eighteen candidates passed in English Language, with one boy gaining a Grade I pass, indicating 75%+ marks. Seven passed in Mathematics, four out of five in cookery, six out of twelve in metalwork, three out of five in needlework and in human biology. One girl passed in eight subjects, including music.

The foundation had been laid for the change to comprehensive education, which began in 1972 with an entry of 250 children who had not been required to sit an entrance examination at 11 years of age.

The whole administrative structure of the school was changed and enlarged to make the House system an effective basis for four groups of pupils with 300–350 children in each house, named after Welsh mountains so dear to our hearts, viz — Aran, Plynlymon, Tryfan and Wyddfa.

The Head of House had responsibilities which could be defined almost as those of a Head Teacher in a small school of 200-300 pupils, and was assisted by a deputy of the opposite sex, and House Tutors, traditionally known in the past as Form Teachers. In this way each child would be a 'known' person in a pastoral foundation which underlaid the whole working of the school.

Each September for five years, we saw a comprehensive intake of some 250 children from the local primary schools. A member of staff had been delegated to act as liaison with these contributories and to develop a meaningful relationship which facilitated the rather traumatic change in the every-day life of the child as it entered a large and often frightening institution. This teacher was designated as Head of Lower School, who together with the Deputy headmaster (Academic Registrar), Deputy Headteacher (Senior Master) and Deputy Headmistress (Senior Mistress) formed a small cabinet with the Head Teacher to deal with the nitty-gritty tasks of running a large school.\In 1977 the change-over to comprehensive was complete. There were 1,380 pupils on roll, a staff of nearly 100 teachers, an office under the direction of a lady registrar, a resources department run by a member of staff assisted by a non-teaching technician, a new Sports Hall, swimming pool, additional classrooms, science laboratories, a language laboratory and what was to become the hub of the new school, a magnificent library.

Twenty years of consistent hard work had seen the laying of a solid educational foundation. It was a tribute to a body of teachers who had one ideal in mind — excellence.

This was the end of the beginning.

Gareth V. Williams
(Headmaster 1957–77)

Mr Gareth Vaughan Williams, the first headmaster of St David's, was a native of Rhosllannerchrugog and was educated at Ruabon Grammar School and Manchester University. After service in the Royal Army Medical Corps during the Second World War he trained as a teacher and served as an assistant teacher of Geography at Deeside Secondary Modern School. When the establishment of St David's was announced he applied for three posts: teacher in charge of Geography, deputy headmaster and headmaster. Gareth Williams, more than any other individual, can be credited with having created the ethos and atmosphere of St David's and was still in post when the major upheaval of comprehensive education became a fact in 1972. He retired in 1977.

This photograph was taken in the original headmaster's office, which later became the medical room. The school's first Tannoy P.A. system can be seen behind him.

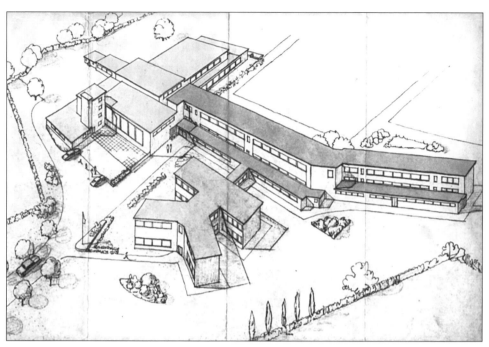

The original artist's impression of how the completed 'Holt Road Secondary School' would look. The name was quickly changed to St David's Secondary School to reflect the sense of Welshness of Wrexham. Designed by the Denbighshire County Architect's Department, the building was typical of the utilitarian design popular in the 1950s. The main classroom block was originally intended to be one straight corridor but land drainage problems meant that it had to be built on a number of concrete rafts and a 'dog-leg' inserted forming separate Central and West Corridors.

The completed Science and Technical block, 1957. The builders have moved out and all that is missing is the grass lawn and the pupils.

Staff, 1958. *Back row:* Mr David Davies (History), Rev Edryd Jones (R.I.), Mr Leslie Griffiths (Maths), Mr Ralph Byrne (Rural Studies), Mr Ray Wilkins (P.E.), Mr Tom Roberts (Maths); Mr Emyr Prys-Jones (Biology), Mr Eddie Hughes (Science). *Middle row:* Mr Cyril Griffin (Metalwork), Mr Geraint Thomas (Welsh), Miss Helen Robinson (Music), Miss Marian Davies (English), Miss Dawn Coates (R. I. & English), Mrs Barbara Davies (P.E.), Miss Pat Hughes (English), Miss Cathy Price (Craft), Mr Ralph Morgan (Remedial), Mr Derek Williams (General Subjects), Mr Jimmy Birchall (Woodwork). *Front row:* Mrs Flint (Supply), Mrs Margaret Ellis (Needlework), Mr Russell Holmes (Art), Mr Gwilym Phillips (Deputy Headmaster/Geography), Mr Gareth Williams (Headmaster), Miss Marjorie Davies (Deputy Headmistress/Cookery), Mr Niall Crane (Maths), Miss Liz Edwards (Remedial), Mr Arthur Clarke (English).

The original St David's School Choir. Photographed in November 1958 with their choir mistress Miss Helen Robinson seated in the centre of the second row. This choir laid the foundations of a musical tradition that was to bring the school's name to the attention of an international audience.

Mr Ralph Byrne with members of his Rural Studies class in the school 'allotments' which are clearly visible on the extreme left of the aerial photograph shown on page 14. Ralph Byrne retired in 1989, the last of the original members of staff.

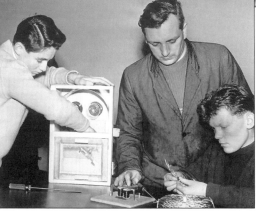

Mr Eddie Hughes teaches the boys the rudiments of electricity in the late 1950s. Mr Hughes joined the staff in September 1958 and retired in 1983.

Aerial photograph of the original schools buildings and grounds.

Pupils in fancy dress costume for the Christmas concert of 1958.

Scottish Dancing party, December 1958.

Below: Christmas Nativity Play, 1958, part of the annual Christmas Concert. This was a forerunner of many notable stage productions by the staff and pupils of St David's School.

1958 class group with their form teacher, Mr Ralph Morgan, a former Royal Marine, who taught at Alexandra School before joining the St David's staff in 1957 as teacher in charge of remedial classes. He later became Senior Teacher and,finally, Deputy Headmaster. He retired in 1983.

1958. A very early photograph of the St David's Rugby squad with Mr Gareth Williams and Mr Tom Roberts.

1958. Mrs Barbara Davies with the school Netball team. Mrs Davies, a native of Monmouthshire, taught in Rugby before re-training as a P.E. teacher at Barry. She taught at Alexandra School, Wrexham from 1956-7 and joined St. David's in October 1957 as P.E. mistress. She retired as Deputy Headmistress in 1980. In 1999, Mrs Davies gained the world 2000 metres Indoor Rowing record for an octagenarian.

Mr David Davies, history teacher, with members of his class, c.1961.

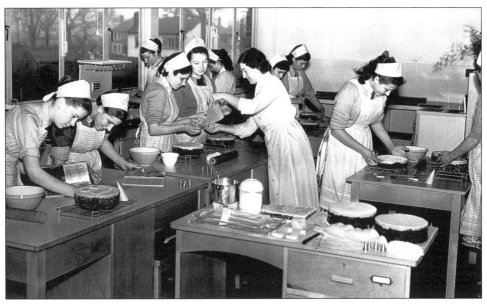

Girls prepare Christmas cakes in the cookery class taken by Miss Marjorie Davies, with not a boy pupil in sight. This classroom was located on the upper floor of what later became the science block.

Name two types of glue.
Answer: Bostick Gule and Evil Stick.

Boys being taught to operate a metalwork lathe by Mr Cyril Griffin. This classroom was located on the ground floor of what later became the science block.

1958.Representative Soccer team. Right: with Mr Niall Crane.

As we stepped outside a strange smell came wafting to my ears.

1958.Representative Soccer team. Left: with Mr Ralph Byrne.

1958.Representative Soccer team. Right: with Mr Russell Holmes.

1958.Representative Soccer team. Left: with Mr Ray Wilkins.

Facing page: Pupils in the School Hall in the early years.

Coached as an extra-curricular activity by Mrs Barbara Davies, Welsh folk dancing proved to be particularly successful with several parties winning high awards in local and national competitions.

The school's first overseas visit occurred in July 1959 when the folk dance group, winners of three National Eisteddfod prizes, travelled to Munich in Germany (accompanied by Mrs Davies and Miss Robinson) to take part in the celebrations commemorating the opening of an international refugee village at Ludwigfeld.

Four teams were invited to attend, representing the four home countries. The costumes were produced in the Needlework Department.

The various national folk dance teams at Munich, 1959. The St David's group are standing to the left of centre.

The original 1957 drawing for the school badge which was designed by Mr Russell Holmes and Mr Macfarlane (County Architect). The badge shows an abbot's mitre, linking the school with Wrexham Abbot and Valle Crucis Abbey, a crozier, symbolic of St David, the key of learning and a motto '*Gorau Dawn Dysg*' (the greatest gift is learning) which was suggested by Alderman Emyr Williams, a member of the Gorsedd of Bards (Emyr Cyfeiliog)

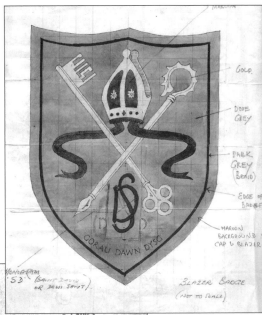

A very poor quality newspaper photograph of the first St David's Swimming Gala, held at Wrexham Baths (Tuttle Street) ,1959.

Another very poor quality newspaper photograph of the school dining room in 1957, accommodated on the stage in the school hall.

Mrs Barbara Davies and Mr Gareth Williams with members of the 1960 Netball team.

Handel's best record is Messiah.

Right: Mr Gareth Williams with the school prefects, *c.*1961. Senior pupils were given positions of authority within the school and house structures. In addition, extra-curricular activities such as sport and assisting with the running of the school library also merited recognition.

Mr Tom Roberts with the Rugby XV, 1962-63.

Extra-curricular activities played an important role in the life of the school from the very first day. In the upper photograph, Mr Arthur King and Mr Ralph Byrne supervise the opening of a beehive with members of the Beekeeping Club. There was an indoor observation hive located in the biology classroom which the bees entered through a hole in the wall seen here.

Left Members of the Chess and Draughts Club while away a lunch hour.

What is a libretto? Answer: A Japanese motor bike.

An early school eisteddfod choir and orchestra.

The Early Years.

The staff were forewarned on the opening day that little, if any, equipment or stationery had been delivered. Some of the furniture had been bought from bankrupt stock and great care had to be taken with the wooden furniture which was likely to give way under daily use. To reduce the movement of pupils, class teaching (when pupils remained in one room and were taught all subjects by their form teacher) was the order of the day for the first few weeks. Pupils largely accepted the standards that were expected of them. There was no need of a tyrannical regime but, correction was available when required, with the headmaster leading from the front. His presence was seen and felt throughout the whole school at all times. Movement was controlled by staff being in the classrooms before the pupils and if the headmaster, a member of staff or a visitor entered a classroom, all the pupils stood as a mark of good manners and were then asked to sit. Litter, both inside and outside the school was almost non-existent and the grounds and buildings were maintained to a high degree of order by the caretaker and groundsman.

The school had 16 classrooms. On the West Corridor were rooms 1–4 (Ground Floor) and 8–11 (1st Floor), the Central Corridor had the Library and rooms 5–7 (Ground Floor) and 13–16 (1st Floor). The central staircase, located between the West and Central Corridors, led to the isolated Room 12. The 'Butterfly Wings' of the Science & Craft Block were approached from the Central Corridor and comprised Biology Lab, General Science Room, Metalwork Room and Woodwork Room (Ground Floor) with the Art Room, Crafts Room, Cookery Room and Needlework Room on the 1st Floor.

Turning left at the main door we approached the Administration Area with the part-time secretary's office (angled Front/Sliding Glass Access), Headmaster's Room (containing the only school telephone and 'Tannoy' school bell and public address system), the Caretaker's Room, School Stockroom and Deputy Headmaster's Room. At the end of the corridor were the female staff toilets, the Medical Room and the male staff toilets. The Staff Room was immediately to the left of the male toilets, overlooking the children's playground. On the left hand side of this corridor was the School Hall with the stage area doubling as a dining hall, off which was located the kitchen.

Four tennis courts were provided across the concreted playground, on the site of the post-1972 Art/Crafts/C.D.T. Block. All other buildings were added to accommodate the changeover to comprehensive education in 1972.

The site of the Sports Hall and Swimming Baths did not belong to the school and was occupied by rows of cottages and a garden nursery area. The present car park was a garden allotment attached to the Gate Hangs High public house. The only cars which appeared regularly in the early days were a Vauxhall (inherited from his father by the Headmaster), an old Rover owned by Mr Clarke and the woodwork master's ancient Morris 8 Tourer (with several wooden embellishments) which was said to have been purchased from the radio comedian Al Read. The only modern car was owned by the school caretaker, a Ford Zodiac or Zephyr finished in a shade of shocking pink! Members of staff were 'spoiled' by having a part of the bicycle sheds reserved for their use.

Despite the difficulties in the early days, these were happy times. Several of the original members of staff have now passed away and, sadly, many of the original pupils. However, there are still multitudes of very happy memories of what was a very happy school, to which staff and pupils contributed so much, as a foundation from which so many others have derived great benefit.

Ralph Byrne Teacher of Rural Studies 1957–72
Head of Newsome Studies 1972–80
Senior Teacher, 1976–89
Head of Resources, 1982 –89

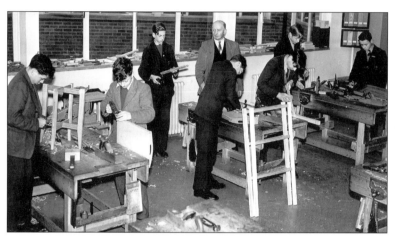

Mr Jimmy Birchall in the woodwork class, located on the ground
floor of what became the Science block) c.1961.

Pupils, teachers (Mrs Barbara Davies and Mr Arthur King) and hotel staff outside the
hotel at Blanes on the Costa Brava, 1963. This was the school's first overseas
holiday with the party travelling from Wrexham to southern Spain by rail.

The original school library, located on the ground floor of the West Corridor (Room 5), was established in 1957 by Mr Arthur Clarke. In later years, with the advent of comprehensive education, the library was moved upstairs into the new building extension and was named the Arthur Clarke Library.

The crowded Staff Room in c.1961. Until 1972, the Staff Room was located at the rear of the School Hall in the room later used by the Music Department. Much of this area of the school was badly damaged in an arson attack in the late 1960s.

The 1962 Girls Athletics Team (right) and the 1962–3 Boys Soccer Team (below). The school came of age in terms of sport in 1962 winning the Wrexham Senior Schools Swimming Gala; Wrexham & District Schools Football Association Under-15 League; Urdd National Football Cup; Aston Cup for Wrexham & District Schools Rugby 7-a-side; Denbighshire Schools Annual Cross-Country (second year in

succession); Wrexham & District Secondary Schools Annual Athletics.

He went up the Leaning Tower of Peaser and dropped feather bricks to prove that objects dropped from the same height take the same time to fall.

Senior Boys Cross-Country team, June 1963. with P.E. teacher Mr Bob Elfed Byrne. A native of Nefyn, Mr Byrne was educated at Pwllheli Grammar School and served for some years in the merchant marine before training at Heath College, Cardiff. He joined the staff of St David's in 1962, became Head of the P.E. Department and retired in 1989.

Staff, July 1960. *Back row:* Mr Harold Williams (Caretaker), Mr Geraint Thomas (Welsh), Rev Edryd Jones (R.I.), Mr Ray Wilkins (P.E.), Mr Les Griffiths (Maths), Mr Ralph Byrne (Rural Studies), Mr Derek Williams (General Subjects), Mr Niall Crane (Maths), Mr Ralph Morgan (Remedial), Mr James Birchall (Woodwork), Mr Arthur Warburton (Groundsman). *Middle row:* Mr Cyril Griffin (Metalwork), Mrs Rose Prothero (Supply), Mr Russell Holmes (Art), Mr David Davies (History), Mr Gareth Williams (Headmaster), Mr Tom Roberts (Maths), Mr Arthur Clarke (English), Mr Gwilym Phillips (Geography), Mr Eddie Hughes (General Science), Mrs Auriel Davies (Geography). *Front row:* Mr Alun Williams (Supernumerary), Miss Dawn Coates (English), Mrs Elizabeth Edwards (Remedial), Mrs Margaret Ellis (Needlework), Miss Sheila Brown (Maths), Miss Marjory Davies (Deputy Headmistress/Cookery), Miss Marian Britland (Crafts), Mrs Edna Griffiths (Secretary), Miss Marian Davies (English), Miss Helen Robinson (Music), Mrs Barbara Davies (P.E.).

Recollections of Mrs Ruth Tindall, an exchange teacher from Deerborn in the U.S.A. who spent a year at St David's in 1961–2.

So many delightfully different memories. I had expected the staff to be what I expected of the British — cool, aloof. Not so. In fact, they were the opposite — warm friendly, full of good humour and quick wit. Particularly fascinating was the headmaster, Mr Gareth Williams. Parents who came to confront a teacher had to get past him (and they never did).

The pupils were so respectful. They stood when called on and called me 'Miss'. Tea time — unheard of in the States. The children were sent to play and the teachers congregated for biscuits and tea — and delightful conversation. But, oh yes, I remember the winter chilblains and how I snuggled up to the heating pipe during class.

Twice a week I played badminton with members of the staff in the evening. It was my first encounter with badminton and … I'm still playing it today [2001] with my fellow retirees.

Best of all were the many warm friends I made at St David's School. I will never forget them.

An important part of the school's philosophy was the recognition of achievement at all levels. This photograph shows the school hall decorated for Speech Day, 1966. The first Speech Day was held in October 1961 when the Director of Education, Mr T. Glyn Davies, was the guest speaker. As the school acquired a reputation for academic success so events such as Speech Day, when the efforts of the pupils were publicly recognised, assumed greater significance.

A regular feature on the school's sporting calendar was the Staff v Boys soccer match. In this 1963 photograph the staff team comprises:
Back row: Mr Bryan Evans. Mr David Meredith, Mr Ray Evans, Mr Dennis Hall, Mr Tom Roberts, Mr Tony Edwards (student), Mr Gareth Green.
Front row: Mr Ralph Morgan, Mr Bob Pugh, Mr Ralph Byrne, Mr Bob Byrne and Mr Russell Holmes.

Right: School Sports Day, c.1963. A young Mr David Meredith records the distances in the boy's long jump. He joined the staff as a probationary teacher in September 1962, became Head of Plynlymon House in 1972 and retired as Deputy Headteacher in 2001. He also served as Acting Headteacher for twelve months in 1998/9.

Below: The school placed great emphasis on outdoor pursuits and encouraged a high level of staff involvement. Mr Jimmy Birchall is assisted with the canoe on the Llangollen Canal.

Right: Even the headmaster was not exempt for extra-curricular activities. Mr Gareth Williams shows 'How it should be done'!

The cast of *Toad of Toad Hall*, which was performed by the pupils on 12 & 13 February 1963. The roles of Mr Toad, Mole and Ratty were taken by ivor Davies, Philip Jones and Angela Roberts. The school's first concert was staged on 17 & 18 December 1957 and quickly became a regular event. The early productions were a combined effort between various departments under the overall control of Mr Arthur Clarke. Costumes were produced by the Needlework classes and sets were designed and constructed by the Art and Woodwork classes.

An attentive History class in the mid 1960s. This was Room 15 which was for many years used as a staff room.

Below: Members of the Chess Club deeply involved in a series of matches against Bryn Alyn School, Gwersyllt, March 1966. This photograph was also taken in Room 15.

An annual 'favourite', the School Cross Country Race gets under-way in Acton Park on a grey winter's afternoon in the late 1960s.

The St David's
School Athletics
team, *c.*1966.

Complete the following similes:
a) As busy as ...   A DOLE QUEUE
b) As safe as ...   THE GREEN CROSS CODE
c) as light as ...   A LIGHT BULB

Left: Girls Gymnastics Team, late 1960s.

Girls Hockey
Team, captained
by Marilyn
Sumpter, *c.*1966.

The cast of *HMS Pinafore* the Gilbert and Sullivan operatic production of March 1967. The main parts were played by Mr Arthur Clarke, Mr Eddie Hughes, Mr Gareth Pugh, Mr Russell Holmes, Mr Wyn Jones, Mrs Margaret Griffiths, Mrs Helen Evans, Gillian Morris and Elaine Dicken.

The School Choir, 1968.

*What is the definition of a Prime
Mover? Answer: A good looking girl.*

School Prefects, 1968–9. *Back row:* Stan Edwards, Martin Clarke, David Camps, Geoff Wilcock, Rob Mahrenholz, Gwynfryn Pritchard, Keith Allmand, Ian Simmons. *Middle row:* Mr Gwilym Phillips, William Jackson, Philip McCann, Dianne Moore, Valerie Simmons, Jennifer Bradbury, Loraine Vaughan, Lynn Hadley, Susan Tunley, Elizabeth Hubbard, Ronnie Thomas, Mr Gareth Williams. *Front row:* Maxine Jones, Pauline Farmer, Ann Owen, Elaine Dicken, Michael Earles, Janet Edwards, Cynthia Howell, Gwenda Evans.

Art class, *c.*1965.

Below: Mrs Margaret Ellis, Miss Marjorie Davies and a party of senior girls wave goodbye on the school drive in 1961 as they depart on a school visit to Paris. Mrs Ellis joined the staff in September 1957 as teacher in charge of needlework (she also taught maths) and retired in 1985 as Head of the the Home Economics Department. Note the school weather station in the background.

Left: School uniform was to be worn by all pupils from the outset. As part of the 'secondary modern not second class' philosophy, the uniform very closely resembled that worn by the pupils in the town grammar schools. In 1957 it comprised maroon blazers, worn with either grey skirts or flannels with blue shirts and blouses, maroon ties and maroon caps or berets. By the 1960s the tie had become two coloured (maroon and silver) and the girls' berets had been replaced by a grey hat with a maroon band. In this photograph, Head Girl Gwenda Evans (centre) models the girls uniform with representatives from Grove Park Girls School and Yale Technical Grammar School.

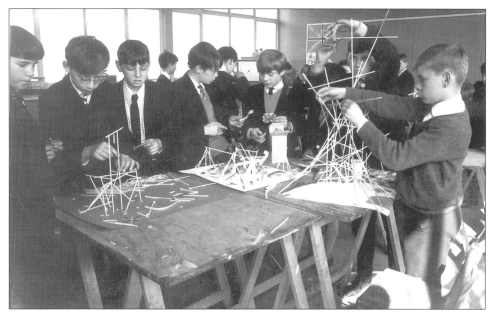

Above: Craft class, *c.*1967

Right: Mr Russell Holmes. After wartime service in the R.A.F., he taught at Llay School before joining the staff of St David's in September 1957 as teacher in charge of art. He is perhaps best remembered for the part he played in the dramatic life of the school, taking leading roles in most of the school and staff productions. He retired in 1982 as a Senior Teacher/Head of Resources.

Left: A house choir competing in the inter-house School Eisteddfod under the leadership of careers master Mr Gareth Green who was himself a leading member of the Rhos Orpheus Choir.

Left: Netball squad, 1968–9.

Above: The sports captains of the winning house hold up the cup at the end of the annual Sports Day in July. Standing behind the desk is Mr Ralph Morgan.

Left: Senior Netball team, 1970–1.

Right: Junior Rugby XV, 1968–9.

The word primitive means they do not have Wembley Football Ground.

Left: Junior Soccer XI, 1969.

Boys' Basketball Team, 1968–9.
Back row: Gwyn Evans, Philip Bagnall, David Armstrong, David Neal, Chris Davies.
Front row: Kevin Davies, David Plack, Neil Whitehand.

The view of the school from the footpath linking Borras Road with Holt Road. The trees fell victim to Dutch Elm disease in the 1970s and were removed to ensure the safety of the pupils. Proposals to replace the trees never came to fruition.

Pirates of Penzance, the Gilbert and Sullivan operatic production was performed by staff and pupils in 1970.

Right: Mr Russell Holmes and Mr Gwynne Belton head the 'police force' comprising David Armstrong, Howard Cash, Richard Chalk, Towyn Cheetham, Roderick Goldswain, Brian Harrison, Nicholas Holmes, Robert McCulley and David Savage.

The Major General's daughters, played by Susan Smith, Gwenda Evans, Joy Edwards, Jane Edwards, Jayne Bullock, Janice Colley, Sian Davies, Dorice Edwards, Linda Jones, Elizabeth Lewis, Linda Manuel, Gillian Painter, June Roberts, Linda Smith, Janet Smith, Lucienne Tomlinson, Enid Williams, Marilyn Williams, Valerie Woodburn and Cheryl Wymer.

The school gymnasium, part of the original 1957 building, it also served as an external examination room after 1972. The door in the back wall led through to the changing rooms.

Left: The Aran House shield, designed by Mr Ralph Morgan. The Head of House in 1972 was Mrs Irene Marshall whose intertwined initials can be seen below the daffodil crest.

Art class, early 1970s.

Prefects and senior pupils, July 1972. Gwilym Phillips (Deputy Headmaster/Geography), Gareth Williams (Headmaster) and Mrs Barbara Davies (Deputy Headmistress/P.E.), with the senior pupils in the final days of St David's Secondary School.

Staff, June 1972. The last pre-comprehensive staff. *Back row:* Mr Underwood (English), Mr Bob Byrne (P.E.), Mr David Meredith (Maths), Mr Tony Williams (Woodwork), Mr Bryan Evans (French), Mr Gerson Davies (R.E.). *Second row:* Mr Arthur King (Biology), Mr Eddie Hughes (Science), Mrs Corinne Evans (Needlework), Mrs Branwen Thomas (Cookery), Mr Gareth Pugh (English), Mr Gareth Green (Maths), Mr Gwynne Belton (History). *Third row:* Mrs Gillian Chalk (Remedial), Miss Mair Phillips (Family Studies), Mrs Barbara McNeil (Special Needs), Mrs Glena Edwards (Welsh), Mrs Helen Evans (Welsh), Mrs Mabel Allanson (Maths), Mrs Gwen Byrne (Remedial), Mrs Sylvia Jones (English), Mrs Sheila Byrne (English), Mrs Judith Clark (Craft), Mrs Sue Seys Llewellyn (P.E.), Mr Les Whitley (General Subjects). *Front row:* Mr Arthur Valentine (Woodwork), Mr Alun Williams (Supernumerary), Mr Arthur Clarke (English), Mr Gwilym Phillips (Deputy Headmaster/Geography), Mr Gareth Williams (Headmaster), Mrs Barbara Davies (Deputy Headmistress/P.E.), Mr Ralph Morgan (Remedial), Mr Cyril Griffin (Metalwork), Mr Ralph Byrne (Rural Studies).

In preparation for the rapid expansion of the school's pupil and staff population, a major building project got underway which resulted in the construction of a new school office, craft rooms, domestic science block, classrooms and the 'Top Corridor'.

In addition, a new sports hall and swimming pool, complete with changing rooms and offices, was built on the east side of the school.

A party of senior girls en route to Stratford on Avon in the 1970s.

Right: The Plynlymon House shield was introduced in 1972. Like all the house shields it was designed by Mr Ralph Morgan.

Left: Members of Mrs Gill Chalk's 2nd year class, 1972. Mrs Chalk trained at Cartrefle College and joined St David's in 1971. She retired in 1985 as Head of Aran House.

Under-15 Soccer Team, winners of the Wrexham & District Under-15 Shield, 1973.
Back: David Williams, Graham Wright.
Middle: Philip Jones, Andrew Paterson, Peter Read, Stephen Lodge, Michael Griffiths, Stephen Goring, Alan Later.
Front: Leigh Richards, Michael Collins, Russell Natt, Gareth Downing (Capt,), Michael Williams, Peter Darlington.

Trip to Beaumaris Castle, July 1970. A party of pupils accompanied by Mr Bob Byrne and Mr Les Whitley.

Left: In the days before overseas travel became commonplace the school organised a number of foreign 'holidays' for pupils. Here a group of pupils relax in the heat on a beach at Lloret de Mar, Spain in 1971.

Right: Mrs Margaret Ellis with pupils on a school 'holiday' to Majorca.

Below: Mr Bryan Evans and a group of pupils examine the route of their cruise on the school ship SS. *Uganda, c.*1973. Mr Evans was from the Moss and graduated from UCNW Bangor before joining the staff in 1962, teaching P.E. and Music. He later became a French teacher and, in 1985, Head of Aran House. He retired in 1996.

The 1974 production of Lionel Bart's *Oliver!* with Gary Conde in the title role. Fagin was played by Mr Russell Holmes, the Artful Dodger by John Blackwell, Bill Sykes by Mr Bryan Evans, Nancy by Mrs Jean Stanley Jones, Mr Bumble by Mr Arthur Clarke and Bet by Michelle Davies. This production, the first after the school became comprehensive, continued the tradition of lavish staff/pupil musicals.

Fagin with his 'gang' of child pickpockets and thieves

Below: Mr Gwynne Belton as the undertaker Mr Sowerberry with Gary Conde (left) and Mrs Helen Evans as Mrs Sowerberry and Mr Arthur Clarke as Mr Bumble.

The chorus and cast of *Oliver!*

Above; The workhouse scene, typical of the elaborate sets designed and built by the school.

Above: Press photograph of Fagin, the Artful Dodger and Oliver Twist.

Right: Nancy (Mrs Jean Stanley-Jones) holds centre stage in the pub scene from *Oliver!*

The school band marches down Regent Street at the head of the annual Round Table Father Christmas Parade. By this time, the band had acquired such a high reputation that it had become the first choice for civic and public events in Wrexham.

Mozart was a podgy child.

The Tryfan House shield introduced in 1972. The dragon in the crest is supporting the letter 'B' for Belton.

Members of the school band who took part in the BBC 'Dial a Carol' programme in 1977. *L–R:* Susan Bray, Ann Griffiths, Susan Edwards, Peter Jones, Simon Blore, Kathryn Gittins, Fiona Matthias.

Welsh International Rugby star, Gerald Davies (46 caps) accompanied by Mr Owain Bale, Mr Bob Byrne and Mr Gareth Williams, addresses the boys in the Sports Hall, 1975. Mr Bale was obviously a 'dedicated follower of fashion'!

In the mid 1970s, Mr Byrne and Mr Bale organised a five-day overseas tour during which two squads (40 boys making up the Under-13s and the Under-14s) were to play three matches against sides from the Avia and Boitsfort Clubs in Brussels, Belgium. As the party crossed the Channel they received news that one of their fixtures had been cancelled. Arriving in Brussels, they were notified that a second fixture was cancelled and, when they turned up for the third match, they discovered that the opposing team was made up of Under-17s and that game was also called off. Not quite the sort of undefeated overseas tour that the boys expected!

Above: Soccer, the winners of the 1975 Wrexham & District Under-13 League and the Clwyd Champions (beating Deeside and the Vale of Clwyd finalists).

Mr Owain Bale, seen here teaching rugby skills to pupils in the late 1970s, was a native of Pontardawe. He trained at Cartrefle College and joined St David's in 1972. He left in 1987 and is currently Deputy Headteacher of St Deiniol's School, Marchwiel.

Ist Year Rugby XV squad which ended the 1974-5 season with an undeafeated record — scoring 200 points and conceding only 18. *Back*: A. Roberts, N. Stennett, S. Jarvis, T. Hughes, N. Allen, Mr Bob Byrne, J. P. Williams, N. Davies, T. Batho, M. Keen, J. Green. *Front*: K. Williams, N. Williams, I, Kyffin, S. Jones (Capt.), N. Edwards, K. Turnbull, C. Williams, N. Jones.

Winners of the Wrexham & District Under-14 Hockey Tournament, March 1975.
Back: Christine Camm, Karen Wright, Fern Middleton, Anne Broughton, Heather Pierce, Karen Bird. *Front:* Yvonne Usher, Joanna Matthias, Karen Young, Carol Davies and Pauline Grice.

All the writers of the Bible were Jewish except one, who was David Kossoff.

St David's Cricket 8-a-side squad, runners up in the county competition, 1975.

Fashion conscious young ladies prepare for the start of the annual school Cross-Country Race in Acton Park, although some appear to have a different method of transport in mind.

Winners of the Enid Daniels-Jones Gymnastics Trophy, November 1975.
Back: Linda Fisher, Jane Coates, Heather Pierce, Angela Phoenix, Deborah Jones, Nora Edwards, Wendy Hoare.
Middle: Anita Ward, Carol Davies, Karen Young, Lynn Jones, Fern Middleton.
Front: Heather Forward.

Wrexham & District Under-16 Basketball Champions, April 1975. *Standing*: D. Snell, K. Spruce, P. Griffiths, A. Phillips, A. Davies.
Front: B. Williams (Capt.), K. Sykes.

The 1976 production of *The Pirates of Penzance* the last of the St David's operettas. The leading roles were taken by: Mr Arthur Clarke, Mr Gareth Green, Mr Bryan Evans, Mr John Morris, Mr Russell Holmes and Mrs Helen Evans.

Above: The police constables: Jonathan Moore, Mr Bob Ellis, Mr Owain Bale, Mr Martin Watson, Mr Chris Stubbs, Mr Dafydd Jones. Front: Mr Gwynne Belton.

Left: Mr Colin Fisher and Mrs Jean Stanley Jones who took the already high standard of music education at St David's to a new level of excellence. Mr Fisher, trained in the Wrexham Salvation Army Citadel Band before going to the University of Bristol. He taught in Manchester before joining the staff in 1972 as Head of Music. Mrs Stanley Jones trained in Birmingham and was appointed to St David's in 1972. She left in 1996 on being appointed music advisor to the four north-east Wales counties. Together they achieved unequalled success with both the School Band and the School Choirs.

The Major General, played by Mr Arthur Clarke, with the 'daughters': Gaenor Mason, Karen Large, Joanne Shields, Susan Bray, Amanda McKay, Kathryn Gittins, Lorraine Cutler, Susan Edwards, Beverly Slawson, Helen Griffiths, Amanda Hughes, Joanna Matthias, Yvonne Usher, Karen Chesworth, Karen Cotton and Christine Chaplin. Mr

Arthur Clarke joined the staff in September 1957 as teacher in charge of English. He founded the school library which, on his retirement in 1976, was named The Arthur Clarke Library. He played a major role in extra-curricular activities, both on the stage and outside of school where, in addition to organising trips to see plays at Stratford on Avon, he was the first organiser of regular field trips to the mountains of north Wales.

Left: The pirates were played by Rev John Jenkins, Mr Eddie Hughes, Mr Dennis Gilpin, Philip Jones, Meirion Matthias, Gareth Hughes, Philip Thomas, Tony Stappleton, Howard Charles, Gary Attard, Peter Jones, Jonathan Simpson, Alan Jones and Ian Kyffin.

Below: Wrexham & District Under-16 Badminton League winners, May 1976. L–R: Nicholas Williams, Johanna Matthias, Michael Wynne, Karen Wright and Rikki Griffiths. In the same year, St David's won the Girls Under-16 Hockey and Netball, Under-14 Netball, Junior Swimming, School's Gymnastics, Under-13 Rugby, Under-13 Soccer (area, league and county champions). Twelve boys were members of the County squad which won the North Wales Soccer Shield.

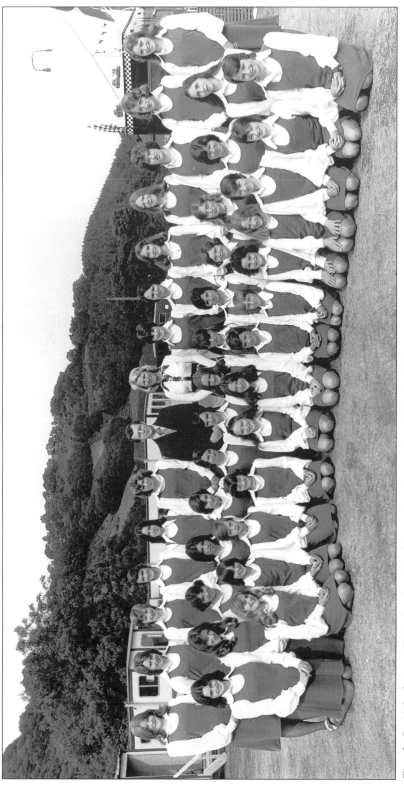

The St David's School Girls Choir at the Llangollen International Musical Eisteddfod, 1976. As the *Liverpool Daily Post* recorded, this choir '... defeated the musical giants of Britain, Germany, the U.S. and Canada to score one of the few major Welsh victories at Llangollen' by beating 21 other contestants in the children's under-16 choir competition. This was only the choir's second year at Llangollen. The Girl's Choir holds the record for points awarded to any children's choir at Llangollen, an amazing 198 points out of a possible 200.

A regular feature of the school in the mid and late 1970s was the Friday afternoon Play Group which met under the supervision of Mrs Rowena Silvester and Mrs Barbara Davies. This allowed the girls to gain some experience of

child care and was an early example of the personal and social education aspect of school life. Julie Harper (above) and Lynn Parry (left).

Right: The Wyddfa House shield, introduced in 1972.

The arrival of the school's second 'bus', a 35-seater Bedford coach, in April 1977. Amongst those present in the photograph are Mark Etchells, Gary Sharp, Lawrence Chalk (Head Boy), Jill Potts (Head Girl), Mr Gareth Williams and Mr Ralph Byrne.

St David's School, 1977–86

From 1977 to 1986 the school was fortunate to build upon the solid foundation established by the inspirational leadership of Mr Gareth Vaughan Williams and staff. As the school grew in numbers (1,450) the pupil intake evolved to become fully representative of the whole community, extending from the Gresford roundabout in the north to the Abenbury brickworks area in the south.

The early academic achievements were further built upon and the curriculum broadened to include new subject areas such as Modern Languages, CDT (Craft, Design, Technology), Information Technology and City & Guilds foundation courses. By 1984, 63% of the pupils gained GCE O-level passes and only 8% left the school with no formal qualifications.

In keeping with its comprehensive ethos, the school pioneered the integration of pupils with physical handicaps into mainstream education. HMIs reported that 'the presence of these pupils has added a significant dimension to the school's caring and it is heartening to witness the consideration, help and support given to them by their peers'. Linked with this development was the opening up of the school swimming pool to the community and, in conjunction with the Wrexham Society for the Handicapped, the building of special changing rooms and facilities to provide disabled access to the swimming pool.

The commitment of the staff to the achievement of the pupils' experience continued through sporting and cultural activities. The school produced successful sports teams in netball, hockey, soccer and rugby, along with an emerging outdoor pursuits activities programme which culminated in the ascent of the highest peaks in England, Scotland and Wales during the weekend of the newly introduced May bank holiday; the resulting sponsorship contributed significantly to the purchase of a new minibus.

On the cultural side, the school gained national prominence in its musical achievements. The choir took first prize for Children's Choirs at the Llangollen International Eisteddfod on no less than five occasions. In addition, the choir took first prize in the International Choral Competition in Montreux, Switzerland. Other prizes include the 'Outstanding Performance Award' at the first ever National Choral Competition held at the Royal Festival Hall and first prize in the BBC Radio 3 international competition 'Let the People Sing'. The school band has twice won the 'Outstanding Performance Award' at the National Festival of Symphonic Wind Bands held at the Royal Festival Hall and has taken first prize at the National Eisteddfod of Wales. HMI deemed the school's music 'noteworthy for its extent, its variety and its outstanding quality'.

In seeking to foster community links the school pursued three avenues: it established itself as one of the largest adult centres in the county, offering a range of Local Education Authority sponsored courses as well as those organised by self-financing groups; it positively encouraged the sharing of its facilities with parents and community groups and pioneered the dual-use of school facilities in the Wrexham area.

The governors and staff were pleased to have Her Majesty's Inspectors confirm in 1985 that:

'the school is a caring and orderly community; so much is clear from the demeanour and conduct of the pupils about the school, from the way in which pupils and staff demonstrate, in their dealings, their respect for one another and for the care they lavished on the physical environment. These commendable and hard-won features result from a clear and almost universal understanding of the school's aims, in which respect for each individual is paramount; the establishment of systems which are designed smoothly and effectively to contribute to the fulfilment of these aims; the positive attitudes which have been cultivated, and diligence with which staff and pupils apply themselves to maintaining what they recognise as an acceptable model'.

Emlyn R. Jones
Headteacher, 1977–86

Mr Emlyn R. Jones. A native of Flintshire, and graduate of the University of Wales, was an assistant teacher of Geography at Mold Grammar School (1965–7). He became Head of Department at the Elfed School in Buckley (1967–71) and Deputy Headmaster at Castell Alyn High School in Hope (1971–7). He was appointed Headmaster of St David's School in 1977. Emlyn Jones left in 1986 on being appointed Principal of Yale VI Form College, Wrexham.

At the end of each year the staff organised an informal 'Theme Evening'. This group at the 1978 French Evening includes Mrs Rowena Silvester, Mrs Brenda Byrne, Mr Ralph Byrne, Mr Oliver Silvester and Mr Glyn Edwards. Other themes were Wild West, Bavarian and Hollywood & TV evenings.

The Out and About Society encouraged pupils to take an interest not only in their own environment but in the world at large. Regular weekly speakers were supplemented by occasional forays into the real world. Here pupils are on a camping expedition to the upper reaches of the Ceiriog Valley, c.1977.

'The management wants to get Butlins to attack the holidaymakers.'

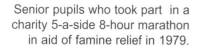

Early signs of things to come. St David's pupil Barbara Jones with an Amstrad micro computer (memory 64k!).

Captain Cook set out to discover the Back Passage and died in the attempt.

Senior pupils who took part in a charity 5-a-side 8-hour marathon in aid of famine relief in 1979.

In 1977, the staff formed an amateur dramatic group called the St David's Players. Their first production was *Ghost Train*, performed in November 1977 followed by *Hobson's Choice* in January 1979.

The Ghost Train, 1977.
Left: Mr Dewi Davies and Miss Diane Meredith (later Mrs Edwards) backstage.
Below: Mr Alister Williams, Mrs Irene Marshall and Mr David Mitchelhill.

Above: Mr Dafydd Jones and Miss Helen Evans.

Above: Rev John Jenkins. Who can forget his exit in Act 2 and return, 30 seconds later, in Act 3?

Above: Mr Arthur Valentine and Miss Pam Roberts (later Mrs Shaw).

Left: Miss Eirwen Williams (later Mrs Vogler) and Mr Bernard Eccles.

Hobson's Choice, 1979. Mr Dafydd Jones, Mr Eddie Hughes and Mr Alister Williams.

Below: This line-up from the cast of *Hobson's Choice* comprises: Mrs Jean Pierce, Mr Dafydd Jones, Mr David Mitchelhill, Rev John Jenkins,

(continued) Mrs Eirwen Williams, Mr Gwynne Belton, Miss Karen Hanley and Mr Russell Holmes. Rev Jenkins held the 'Peculiar' living of Bersham and, after leaving St David's in 1982 became Anglican Vicar of Tenerife. Mrs Pierce retired in 1990 and Miss Williams later taught history at Flint and Yale College.

Left: Mr Russell Holmes as Henry Hobson and Mr Gwynne Belton as Jim Heeler in a scene from *Hobson's Choice*. Mr Belton was trained at the Normal College, Bangor and taught on the Wirral and in Brynteg before joining St David's staff in 1967 as a member of the history department. He became Head of Tryfan House in 1970, a post which he held until 1986 when he became Head of Careers Education. He retired in 1993.

Q: Define 'Occupational Hazard'.
A: Mr Belton is an Occupational Hazard to being a pupil in this school.

Winners of the Girls Open Gymnastics Competition at the National Eisteddfod, Wrexham, 1977.

Netball Team, *c.*1980.

Below: In the late 1970s St David's tennis players won the Clwyd league championship at under-13 and under-15, the individual winner and runners-up in the under-14 group and the under-14 and under-16 doubles championships.

L–R: Patrick Hughes, Julian Aby, David Hawke, John Sellwood, James Slater, Stuart Yarwood, Gerald Palmer, Martin Hallam and Mark Fisher.

Mr Fisher and the School Band perform at Erddig in the late 1970s.

Left: Mrs Margaret Ellis and pupils receive a cheque from NatWest awarded in recognition of the school's Help the Aged project. After 1972, the school tie was silver with a narrow maroon stripe and decorated with the school badge in maroon and gold.

Below: A number of senior citizens were invited into school to meet the pupils and pass on their skills, particularly in needlework.

Staff, April 1980 *Back row:* Mr Tony Williams (C.D.T.), Mr John K. Davies (Special Needs), Mr Gareth Green (Careers), Mrs Gill Chalk, Mrs Melvina Roach (Welsh), Mr Chris Stubbs (Drama), Mr John Williams (Geography), Mr Geraint Dodd (Business Studies), Mr Alister Williams (History), Mr Phil Shaw (Physics), Mr Cliff Thomas (Biology), Miss Karen Hanley (English), Miss Kathleen Williams (R.E.), Mrs Ann Jones (English), Mr Dennis Gilpin (Physics), Mr Eddie Hughes (Physics). *2nd row:* Mr Les Whitley (General Subjects), Mr David Mitchelhill (Maths), Mr Dafydd Jones (Computer Studies), Mr Keith Morgan (Art), Mr Bryan Evans (French), Rev John Jenkins (R.E.), Mrs Luned Ainslie (Welsh), Miss Diane Meredith (Drama), Mr Glannaw Jones (Baths Supervisor), Mr Bruno Sznerch (C.D.T.), Mr Philip Jones (C.D.T.), Mr Alwyn Rogers (C.D.T.), Mr Paul Landing (Latin), Mr Owain Bale (P.E.), Mr Bob Byrne (P.E.). *3rd row:* Mrs Rebecca Ennion (Chemistry), Miss Marjorie Apter (French), Mrs Elizabeth Jenkins (History), Miss Margaret Shearn (French), *[Continued on next page]*

[Continued from facing page] Mrs Noreen Thomas (French), Mrs Mabel Allanson (Maths), Mrs Sheila Williams (Maths), Miss Sue Collins (English), Mr Trevor Roberts (Special Needs), Mr Gareth Hewitt (Geography), Mr Ray Ingham (Gen. Science), Mr Preston Armstrong (Tech. Drawing), Mr Colin Fisher (Music), Mrs Jean Stanley Jones (Music), Mrs Edna Griffiths (Admin. Officer). *4th row:* Mrs Margaret Ellis (Needlework), Mrs Jean Pierce (Maths), Mrs Jenny Board (Art), Miss Helen Evans (Cookery), Mrs Elizabeth Wynn Jones (Welsh), Miss Heather Offord (Needlework), Miss Erica Rudall (Biology), Mrs Pam Shaw (P.E.), Mrs Mair Williams (P.E.), Mrs Angharad Jurkiewiz (Special Needs), Mrs Valerie Conway (Secretary), Mrs Beryl Winn (School Meals), Mrs Nesta Holmes (Nurse), Mrs Gwen Harris (Canteen Supervisor). *5th row:* Mrs Margaret Slade (Nursery Assist,), Miss Vivienne Jones (Resources Tech.), Mrs Barbara Willoughby (Secretary), Mrs Rene Jackson (Asst. Secretary), Miss Irene Burton (Nursery Assist.), Mrs Valerie Williams (English), Mrs Rowena Silvester (Geography), Mrs Eileen Sanham (English), Miss Andrea Hamilton (English), Mrs Mary Evans (English), Mrs Helen Evans (Careers), Mrs Menna Tompkinson (Art), Mrs Marilyn Bell (Lab. Assist.). *Front row:* Mr Ralph Byrne (Geography), Mr Tony Edwards (Maths), Mr Russell Holmes (Art), Mr Gwynne Belton (History), Mr Ralph Morgan (Deputy Headmaster), Mr Emlyn Jones (Headmaster), Mrs Barbara Davies (Deputy Headmistress), Mr David Williams (Deputy Headmaster), Mr David Meredith (Maths), Mr Glyn Edwards (Geography), Mrs Irene Marshall (English).

St David's 1st Year Boys, winners of the Wrexham & District Schools Athletics competition. *L–R:* Nicholas Chidley, Richard Price, Jason Jones, Sean Roberts, Stephen Ford, Richard Williams, Simon Edwards and Andrew Hughes.

Mr Les Whitley and Mr Owain Bale with a group of pupils in the French Pyrenees, 1978. Mr Whitley, a former member of the Palestine Police Force and employee of MANWEB was a late entrant into teaching, joining the staff of St David's as a General Studies teacher straight from Cartrefle College in the late 1960s. His amiable and witty personality made him popular with both staff and pupils

Under-15 Netball Team, October 1979, which won the Wrexham Area Netball Tournament.
Carole Ditchfield, Jayne Belton, Jane Davies, Valerie Bates, Melanie Jones, Wendy Binnersley, Julie Evans, Tracy Hale, Carolyn Rogers.

Right: Junior Girls Athletics Team, May 1980 which won the Miss Violet Brown Trophy at the Wrexham Maelor District School Sports. Back row: Alison Edwards, Judith Williams, Tracy Hughes, Mandy Pickup, Fay Binnersley, Jane Evans. Front row: Karen Adams, Amanda Galloway (Capt.), Kay Lambert Evans.

Below: School Hockey Squad, April 1979.

A Victorian Evening, comprising the play *Maria Marten — Murder in the Red Barn,* was performed in 1980 by the pupils as part of a music hall/ melodrama evening. The role of compère was taken by David Crawford.

The dramatic finale to *Maria Marten,* the execution of William Corder (Timothy Saiet).

In addition to the main dramatic production, the evening also gave individual pupils the opportunity to perform sketches and variety acts. *Left,* David Crawford and Diane Cooper perform *When Father Papered the Parlour* and *above,* Andrew Barker and Stephen Davies perform *Sam Hall.*

Mr & Mrs Marten (Andrew Jones and Helen Davies) in a scene with Maria (Susan Parry) and Tim Bobbin (Mark Pemberton).

Above right: The Head of Drama, Mr Chris Stubbs (right) was a driving force behind many of the major school productions. After a career in the RAF and the Police, Chris Stubbs trained at Cartrefle College and UCNW Bangor and joined the staff at St David's in 1972. He retired in 1987.

The musical direction was provided by Mr Colin Fisher (orchestra) and Mrs Jean Stanley Jones (choir).

Catherine Rees sings *Waiting at the Church.*

The Prince and Princess of Wales meet the school choir at Deeside during their post-wedding tour of Wales, 1981.

Left: The School Band on stage at the Royal Festival Hall, London, 1986.

Right: It was a hard life being a teacher in the 1980s. Heads of House Mr Gwynne Belton and Mr Glyn Edwards, spare no energy to urge their respective houses on to success in the annual Sports Day, July 1983. After wartime service in the RAF, Glyn Edwards was appointed a teacher at Pentredwr before moving to Brynteg and finally to St David's in 1972 He retired in 1983.

Snowdon became popular when the Llanelli Railway went to the top of Mount Everest.

Left: A party of pupils on a field visit to Yorkshire in the early 1980s, accompanied by Mr Les Whitley and Mr Gareth Hewitt.

Indicative of the good humour which existed between staff and pupils was this cartoon, drawn by David Jones of 5T2 in 1982. For many years it hung in the Staff Room and still provokes great interest and humour nearly twenty years later. The individual members of staff are identified overleaf.

Airborne: Mr Paul Landing. *Centre:* Mr Paul Davies. *Back row:* Mr Gareth Green; Mr Alister Williams; Mr Gwynne Belton; Mr Donnally; Mr Barry Cook; Mr J. K. Davies; Mr Preston Armstrong; Mr Colin Fisher; Mr Keith owen; Mrs Menna Tomkinson; Mrs Betty Wynn-Jones; Miss Myers; Mrs Joan Pugh; Miss Andrea Hamilton. *Middle Row:* Mr Paul Nolan; Mr David Mitchellhill; Mr Chris Stubbs; Mr Graham Edwards; Mr Dafydd F. Jones; Mr Bryan Evans; Mr Emlyn Jones; Mr John Williams; Mr Geraint Dodd; Mr Ralph Byrne; Mr Les Whitley; Mrs Jenny Board; Mrs Eileen Sanham; Mrs Gillian Chalk; Mrs Becky Ennion. *Front row:* Mr Owain Bale; Mr Steve Loring; Mr Gareth Hewitt; Mr Russell Holmes; Mr Tony Edwards; Mr Bob Byrne; Mr Glyn Edwards; Mr Cliff W. Thomas; Mr Don Wells; Rev John Jenkins; Mr Dennis Gilpin; Mr Len King; Mrs Luned Ainslie; Mrs Rowena Silvester; Mrs Jean Stanley-Jones.

The Girl's Choir, led by Mrs Jean Stanley Jones, perform in
the caves at Balve, Germany in 1980.

Members of 5T1 pose on their last official day in school, May 1982.

Radio 1 disk-jockey Mike Reid (in cap and gown) with the St David's team that won the national BBC Top of the Pops Quiz competition.

Al Capone sold home brew kits during the Depression.

Tryfan senior pupils, members of 5T1 and 5T2 pose for a group photograph with Head of House Mr Gwynne Belton, Deputy Head of House Mrs Rowena Silvester, form teachers Mr Keith Owen, Mr Alister Williams and Mr Geoff Coates (extreme right), 1984.

A group of staff (plus one interloper) pose for a souvenir photograph at Newfield Hall. *Back:* Mr Les Whitley, Mr Gwynne Belton, Mrs Pauline Preston, Mr John Clutton, Mr Gareth Hewitt. *Front:* Mrs Gillian Williams, Miss Stella Wilson, Mrs Sylvia Jones, Mr Owain Bale.

74

Pupil: I did not realise that it was possible to walk uphill all day, never go downhill, and still end up where you started from!

Great emphasis was always placed upon outdoor pursuits from the very earliest days and Mr Arthur Clarke and Mrs Margaret Ellis organised an annual hike to the top of Snowdon. In the 1980s the Humanities Faculty became one of the driving forces of curriculum development in St David's. Among the many innovations introduced at this time were regular field visits for both senior and junior pupils. In the above photograph, Mr Gareth Hewitt, Head of Faculty, leads a group of pupils on a Geography field visit to Yorkshire. Mr Hewitt left in 1985 to become Deputy Head of Ysgol Rhiwabon.

Left: A party of senior geography pupils pause on a hot summer's day on Helvellyn in the Lake District. The field visits, although enjoyed by all pupils, were always both physically and educationally demanding and could never be described as a 'jolly'.

A group of junior pupils with Mrs Pauline Preston, Mrs Gillian Williams and Mrs Brenda Humphreys at Newfield Hall during a field trip to Malhamdale, Yorkshire.

In 1975 St David's became the first school in Clwyd to admit a handicapped pupil into mainstream education. The pilot scheme ran successfully and a second pupil arrived two years later.

By the mid 1980s the small, integrated group of disabled pupils were playing an important part in the day-to-day life of the school. *Above:* the St David's 'Squad' at the Welsh National Disabled Mini-Games, Llandudno, June 1984.

Above: Nicky Holland competing in the wheelchair event at Llandudno.

Left: The canteen at the BICC factory which was decorated for Christmas 1984 by the St David's pupils.

Below: Mr Paul Davies and Mr Steve Loring (back to camera) with pupils at a residential

(continued) outdoor pursuit course at Broadhaven, Dyfed in 1985. Mr Loring joined St David's in 1975 as an assistant teacher of Chemistry. In the early 1990s he retrained as a teacher for the Hearing Impaired. Mr Paul Davies joined the Science Department from St Joseph's RC School and later became teacher in charge of outdoor pursuits.

Above: Mrs Mair Williams with the Hockey Squad, winners of the Wrexham & District Hockey Tournament in the early 1980s.

Right: A group of wildly enthusiastic looking senior pupils on a geology field trip to Borth, Ceredigion in the early 1980s — 'If you don't feel the pain, you don't get the gain'.

Junior Rugby squad, *c.*1986.

The Girls Choir, lead by Mrs Jean Stanley Jones and accompanied by Mr Colin Fisher, en route to victory in the 1984 Montreux Festival in Switzerland.

The Science Faculty staff at the time of the retirement of Mr Dennis Gilpin, 1985. *Back row:* Mrs Pat Brown, Andrew Coleclough, Mike Surtees, Paul Davies, John Pritchard, Steve Loring, Marilyn Bell. *Front row:* Mrs Cath Morris, Mrs Pauline Preston, Dennis Gilpin, Mrs Brenda Humphreys, Mrs Becky Ennion.

The retirement of Mrs Mary Evans (Head of English) and Mrs Gillian Chalk (Head of Aran House), 1985. *L–R:* Mrs Noreen Thomas, Miss Margaret Shearn, Mrs Mary Evans, Mrs Gillian Chalk, Mrs Jean Pierce, Mrs Marjorie Morris and Mrs Rowena Silvester.

St David's School, 1986–2003

In 1986 St David's was a fine school in a different time. Throughout the years that followed it was proud to be both successful and respected. A great many changes occurred, both in society and in education, and there was much to celebrate. The years since 1986 have been about successfully managing the challenges of change while preserving the important aspects in the school.

During this time there was something unique about St David's; a character and quality that was apparent to everyone. Part of it was reflected by the motto 'Care, consideration and respect', part by the very high standards achieved by the pupils and part by the loyalty and affection of both pupils and staff. This uniqueness was seen not only in what was done, but also in the way in which it was done. Both visitors and school inspectors saw it straight away, and the 1997 HMI Report tried to pin it down, stating that they had found 'A good school with many fine features' which included:

- ° 'The quality of teaching is a strength of the school'
- ° 'The motto 'Care, consideration and respect' powerfully influences pupils' moral and social development'
- ° 'The school has developed a strong ethos and identity as a community'
- ° 'The school has an outstanding reputation for its music'

Throughout this time people, and their achievements, were valued.

Perhaps the above reasons are why the closure of the school is something to celebrate! A concert, two services at St John's Church, an exhibition, a book, a pupil's publication and a Fun Day. It is a time to remember with affection the success, the relationships and the achievements.

Why was the character of the school like this? It was the product of the people who were there: the pupils who were proud to be members of the school and gave of themselves positively and openly, they were its foundation; the Governors were vital, always excellently led — Cllr Beresford, Mr Dennis Francis, Dr Alex Wright and Mrs Christine Whiles guided the school through challenging and changing times in their role as Chair; the teaching and non-teaching staff were central — too many to mention individually, but each making a great contribution. Few members of staff left! St David's was a school that we all enjoyed being a part of, and working in for some considerable time. We came to know, and be known by, generation after generation of our local community.

We are proud to end as the school had begun.

Geoffrey Rate
Headteacher, 1986–2003

Mr Geoffrey Rate, a native of Ilford, Essex, was educated at Wanstead County High School, London and Goldsmith's College. He began his working career in Somerset with the Clarks shoe company. He taught in Essex, the London Boroughs of Redbridge and Haringey before being appointed Deputy Head of Rhyl High School. He became Headteacher at St David's in 1986.

Form group 1T1 in their Science lesson, 1986.

Below: A group of Wyddfa 5th Year pupils pose with House Tutor Mr Chris Stubbs and Head of House Mrs Luned Ainslie, *c.*1987.

Staff, July 1987. *Back row:* Mr Stephen Murray (Geography), Mr Keith Owen (German), Mr Dafydd Jones (Maths), Mr John K. Davies (Special Needs), Mr Borhan Hashemi (Maths), Mr Don Wells (Resources), Mr Gwynne Belton (History), Mr Barry Cook (English), Mr Tony Williams (C.D.T.), Mr Nigel Davies (Maths), Mr John Wenlock (C.D.T.), Mr Noel McKeand (P.E.), Mr Tony Edwards (Maths), Mr Steve Loring (Chemistry), Mr George Sumner (C.D.T.). *2nd row:* Mr Jim Daley (E.W.O.), Mrs Rowena Silvester (Geography), Mrs Gillian Williams (R.E.), Mrs Barbara Willoughby (Admin. Officer), Mrs Eileen Williams (Admin.), Mrs Jenny Board (Art), Mrs Carys Ingham (Welsh), Mrs Helen Evans (Careers), Mrs Barbara Wynne (Home Economics), Miss Delyth Jones (Admin.), Mrs Tracey Rogers (Resources Technician), Mrs Sylvia Jones (History), Miss Lorainne Ryan (Home Economics), Mr Andrew Coleclough (Physics), Mr John Williams (Geography), Mr Bruno Sznerch (C.D.T.), Mr John Pritchard (Physics), Mr Ralph Byrne (Geography). *3rd row: Mr* Graham Edwards (Welsh), Mr Colin Fisher (Music), Mr Michael Hand (Art), Mr David Mitchelhill (Maths), Mr Ken Brown (USA Exchange, History), Mr Geraint Dodd (Business Studies), Mr Alister Williams (History), Mr John Clutton (Deputy Headmaster), Mrs Margaret Slade (Nursery Assist.), Miss Stella Wilson (English), Mrs Eileen Sanham (English), Mrs Noreen Thomas (French), Mrs Marjorie Morris (French). *Front row:* Mrs Siân Rogers (Cookery), Mrs Diane Owen (Special Needs), Miss Andrea Hamilton (English), Miss Avril Howarth (English), Mrs Pauline Preston (Science), Mrs Pat Brown (Science), Mrs Marilyn Bell (Lab. Technician), Miss Margaret Shearn (French), Mr Geoffrey Coates (History), Mrs Joan Pugh (Deputy Headmistress), Mr Geoffrey Rate (Headmaster), Mrs Brenda Humphreys (Maths), Mr Len King (Maths), Mrs Janice Westwood (English), Mrs Ann Caldicott (English), Mr David Meredith (Maths), Mrs Luned Ainslie (Welsh), Mrs Diane Edwards (Drama).

Netball, *c.*1989. Mrs Mair Williams with the Netball Squad. Mrs Williams, a native of Pentredwr, Llangollen, trained at Staffordshire Training College and taught for a number of years at Bryn Offa School before joining St David's in 1976. She guided numerous teams of girls to district, regional and national success in a variety of sports. She became Head of Physical Education and and retired in 1995.

Sir Thomas More was a Spitfire pilot in the Second World War who had both his legs amputated through a crash in the aircraft.

Left: A group of 5th Year pupils at the RAF Museum on the annual History trip to London during the 1980s.

A group of Tryfan House staff, *c.*1988. *L–R:* Mr Alister Williams (House Tutor), Mr Bruno Sznerch (Deputy Head of House), Mr George Sumner (House Tutor), Mrs Carys Ingham (Head of House).

Facing page: One of the major events of the school year was the Work Experience Week. In September of each year the 5th Year pupils were placed with local companies to gain a taste of 'real life'. This was an enormous logistical problem for the Head of Careers who had to locate up to 250 placements and visit every pupil in his/her place of work. The whole project was very successful and pupils gained a great deal from their week away from school as witness the faces on the photographic montage reproduced opposite. Clockwise from the top left-hand corner: Sharon Griffiths, Clare Lush, Claire Jones, Rachel Thomas at Barkers Lane CP School, 1988; Emma Bendon at Clapper Farm, 1989; Joanne Binyon at the Pathology Lab, Maelor Hospital, 1991; Julian Johnson at Wrexham Golf Club; Sharah Preston at Wrexham Lager, 1989; Andrew Richardson with Clwyd Forestry, 1991; Jonathan Everall at Barkers Lane CP School, 1991; Mary White and Cherul Hinton at Chronicle Newspapers, 1992; Robert Williams at Kelloggs; Keli Evans and Clare Thomas at Pizza Chef, 1989. Centre (Top–bottom): Lee Barnes at Deggy's Fishing Shop, 1989; Donna Thomas at Hafod-y-Wern Infants School, 1991; James Wheeler at Tescos, 1988.

In 1990, Mrs Margaret Slade, the school's longest serving nursery assistant, published *One Step at a Time*, a personal record of how the school integrated handicapped pupils into mainstream education.

What is it called when a government takes over an industry and runs it on behalf of the people? Answer: Thieving.

Below: Winners of the Wrexham & District Netball Tournament *c.*1995.
L–R: Paula Griffiths, Clare Jones, Bethan Clutton (Capt.), Araceli Dutton, Sarah Kelly, Sally Roberts, Naomi McKay, Rachel Roberts, Rachel Moore, Mrs Mair Williams.

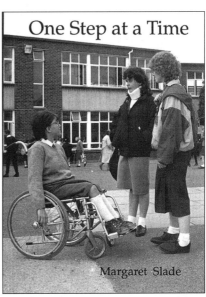

One Step at a Time

Margaret Slade

Mrs Becky Ennion's 5th Year Science Class *c.*1989. Mrs Ennion, a graduate of UCNW Bangor, joined the staff in 1977 and left in 2002 as Head of the Science Faculty to take up an appointment as Teaching & Learning Science Advisor for Wrexham.

Stable equilibrium of a body is obtained when he stands upright and legs slightly apart.

Right: Pupils experimenting with a Van de Graaff Generator under the supervision of Mr John Pritchard in the Physics Laboratory, *c.*1989.

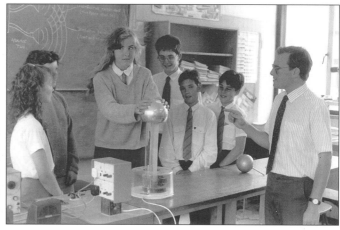

Winners of the Wrexham & District Athletics shield, *c.*1992.

Miss Lisette Nicholls, Mrs Marjorie Morris and Mr Bryan Evans with members of a French class. Mrs Morris (née Apter), a native of Chirk, graduated from UCNW, Bangor and began teaching at Grove Park Girls Grammar School before joining St David's as Head of the French Dept in 1972. She became Head of the Communications Faculty in 1987.

'The Venus de Milo is a French film star.'

The French Department visited Brittany, France in 1995.
Right: Pupils outside the local Tourist Office.
Below: Mr Iain Farquharson, Mr Bryan Evans, Mrs Julia Roberts, Mrs Morris and pupils resting at Mers les Baines.

Mr Colin Fisher introduces the St David's School Band to HM The Queen and HRH the Duke of Edinburgh in 1998 on the occasion of the opening of Wrexham Waterworld.

Certainly worthy of an anthropological study, the 5th Year leaving ritual dance. This, along with a variety of other 'traditional' activities formed part of the annual Rights of Passage for 5th Year pupils on their last full day in school in May.

Mr Tony Williams with pupils in the IT room, c.1999. Tony Williams, a native of Wrexham, trained at Shorditch College, London and joined the staff in 1970 from Speke Comprehensive, Liverpool, as an assistant teacher of woodwork. He became head of the CDT Faculty in 1984, Senior Teacher in 1987 and Assistant Headteacher in 2001.

Pupils at work in the Library Resource Centre, c.1998.

Design Technology pupils (with members of the Rotary Club of Wrexham) putting the finishing touches to bird boxes which were distributed in the local area. St David's were winners of the Rotary Youth & Community Service Cup in 1994 (School Band & Choir) and 1995 (Community Service)

'Joan of Arc has a fire burning under it and eight lanes of traffic.'

A group of pupils on a French Department visit to Paris, 2000.

Mr Colin Fisher conducts the Girl's Choir at the Llangollen
International Eisteddfod, 1999.

Left: Mrs Jenny Board with
Year 7 pupils in the Art
Room. Mrs Board, from Cefn
Bychan, took her degree at
Manchester College of Art
and taught at Chorlton High
School before joining St
David's in 1972. She became
Head of Art in 1988 and was,
for many years, responsible
(originally with Mrs Barbara
Davies) for organising the
Talking Newspaper for the
Blind.

Mr Iain Farquharson
with a group of senior
history pupils, *c.*2000.
Mr Farquharson, who
hails from Kirkaldy in
Scotland, joined the
staff in 1992 and
became Head of
History in 2002.

French visit to Bayeux, Normandy, early 1990s. Staff present are: Mr Bruno Sznerch, Mrs Sylvia Jones and Mr Bryan Evans.

Q: What did Jesus say to John the Baptist after he had been baptised? A: Thanks.

Right: Pupils busily at work in an R.E. examination class during the 1990s.

Q: When the Prodigal Son returned home, who was sorry? A: The fatted calf.

Pupils organising a collection of food for distribution to the local Kids 4 Kidz charity, 1999.

Pupils on a variety of educational visits as part of the Religious Education Department during the 1990s.

Left: Visiting the Law Courts, The Strand, London.

Right: Girls with their heads covered (with the exception of Mrs Pam Massey, standing) sit in the women's area of the Hindu Temple in Birmingham.

'Lourdes is famous for cricket matches.'

Right: Two pupils pledge eternal devotion to each other as part of a mock Jewish wedding at the R.E. Festival held in St David's, *c.*1996.

Pupils sit in the pews at the Manchester Museum & Synagogue.

A picture that encapsulates the school to so many pupils and staff. Two senior pupils, Richard Edwards and Anna Capelen, walk up the drive in the early 1990s, passing the weeping willow tree planted back in 1957 in front of the original school buildings.

'A fully grown tree can break wind for up to 40 metres.'

Right: Miss Nicky Cotter supervises pupils conducting a chemistry experiment in the late 1990s.

Q: What happened to Adolph Hitler? A: He shot himself in the mouth his garage in New York — much to his own distaste.

Lunch 'alfresco' in the area between the School Hall and the Canteen.

One of the less attractive traditions of the senior pupils, whether Fifth Year or Year Eleven, was the autographing of shirts blouses and ties on their final day.

The Black Hole of Calcutta was when 100 men were locked in a room with only one widow — only 23 came out alive.

Above: The School Hall at St David's was designed to accommodate the original pupil population of some 500 boys and girls. As a consequence it later became impossible to hold assemblies for the entire school and morning services were normally organised on a house or year basis.

Mr Bruno Sznerch explains the intricacies of a technology project to a Year 11 pupil. Mr Sznerch joined the staff in 1978 from Mold Alun School and became Head of CDT Faculty. He also served as Deputy Head of Plynlymon House and Tryfan House.

Mrs Barbara Wynne with pupils who have just been awarded the Foundation Certificate in Food Hygiene, October 2002. Mrs Wynne, a native of Wrexham, trained at Radbrook College, Shrewsbury and began her teaching career in Scotland Road, Liverpool before joining St David's in 1966 as an assistant teacher of domestic

science. After a break between 1971 and 1980 she returned and became Head of the Home Economics Department, Head of Aran House and, more recently, Head of Year.

Q: What is the food value of milk?
A: 20p.

Left: Mr Fisher conducts the School Band at the Achievement Day, 2001.

A series of overseas visits to modern historical sites were instituted by the History Department in the 1990s.
Right: Pupils in St Wenceslas Square, Prague, Czech Republic.

Staff, March 2003.

Back Row: Mr David Shaw (Chemistry), Mr Iain Farquharson (History), Mr Nigel Mann (Chemistry), Ms Lesley Whitaker (L.S.A.), Miss Catherine Lindup (Admin. Asst.), Mr Steve Loring (Hearing Impaired), Mr Gareth Roberts (History), Mr Iain Evans (L.S.A.), Mr Paul Davies (Chemistry), Mr Barry Cook (English), Mr Dave Norman (P.E.), Mr George Sumner (D.T.), Mr David Roberts (P.E.), Mr Phil Jones (D.T.), Miss Laura Keel (Admin. Asst.), Mrs Philippa Howe (Biology), Mr Mark Jones (Maths).

2nd Row: Mr Colin Fisher (Music), Mr John Henry (Student), Mr Gareth Wilson (P.E.), Miss Mary Jones (L.S.A.), Mrs Jen Edwards (Maths), Mrs Loraine Hughes (Biology), Mr Des O'Sullivan (English), Mrs Claire Ballamy (P.E.), Ms Laura Calvert (Art), Mrs Alison Ashley (Maths), Mr John Pritchard (Physics), Mr Mike Hand (Art), Miss Laura Salisbury (L.S.A.), Mrs Heather Manhire-Dover (English), Mrs Sue Jones (Special Needs Co-ordinator), Mr Bruno Sznerch (D.T.), Mr David Meredith (Maths), Mr Bryn Rees (Drama).

3rd Row: Mrs Eileen Sanham (English), Miss Alishia Burke (Supply), Mrs Sarah Tiley (Admin. Asst.), Mrs Lyn Davies (Welsh), Mrs Pam Massey (R.E.), Mrs Barbara Wynn (D.T.), Mrs Lyn Jones (Geography), Mrs Brenda Humphreys (Maths), Mrs Diane Rawlinson (L.S.A.), Mrs Helen Carlton (English), Miss Siân Jones (L.S.A.), Mrs Janet Williams (L.S.A.), Mrs Sue Owen (I.T.), Mrs Moira Gaade (D.T.), Mrs Jane Roberts (L.S.A.), Mrs Georgina Mason (French), Mrs Marjorie Morris (French). *Continued facing page.*

4th Row: Mrs Jean Lloyd (Maths), Miss Donna Edwards (P.E.), Miss Lisette Nicholls (N.N.E.B.), Mrs Mary Evans (L.S.A.), Mrs Re Davies (L.S.A.).
Front Row: Mrs Jenny Board (Art), Mrs Cath Moore (Speech & Language), Mrs Eileen Thomas (E.S.W.), Mrs Carys Ingham (Welsh), Dr Luned Ainslie (Welsh), Mrs Sylvia Jones (English), Mr Rob Ratcliffe (Deputy Headteacher), Mr Geoffrey Rate (Headteacher), Mr John Williams (Geography), Mr Tony Williams (I.T.), Mr Adrian Harrison (Admin. Officer), Mr Tony Edwards (Maths), Mrs Barbara Sweetman (N.S.P.C.C.), Miss Claire Wootton (Admin. Asst.), Mrs Marilyn Bell (Lab. Tech.), Mrs Linda Roberts (English).

Year 10 pupils, accompanied by Mr Farquharson, Mr Meredith and Miss Donna Edwards, visit the grave of 'Hedd Wyn', the crowned bard of the 1917 National Eisteddfod, at Artillery Wood Cemetery, Ieper, Belgium, 2003.

Left: Year 10 pupils and staff, pay a silent tribute at the memorial to the Welsh Division, Mametz Wood, Somme, France, 2003.

Year 11 pupils at the memorial to the victims of the Lidice massacre, Czech Republic, 2003.

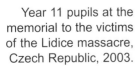

Leaving Prom, May 2003. In the last years of the school, Dr Luned Ainslie organised a Leaving Prom for Year 11 pupils at the Cross Lanes Hotel. Pupils all wore evening dress and enjoyed an event which consisted of a buffet, a disco and a live band.

Dr Ainslie also established a link with Gordonstoun School in Scotland and a number of pupils have been awarded scholarships to attend as members of the VIth Form. Luned Ainslie was educated at Grove Park Girls Grammar School, UCNW, Bangor and the Universities of Manchester and Liverpool. She taught at Welshpool High before joining St David's as Head of Welsh in 1972. She became Head of Wyddfa House in 1983 and Head of Year in 1999.